MOROCCO; OCTOBER 1932:

IT'S *HERE*.

SIX HUNDRED MILES WEST OF *CAPE VERDE*.

THIS IS WHERE I WANT YOU TO *TAKE* US, CAPTAIN BORGES. THIS IS WHERE THE *ISLAND* IS.

WELL, I'M NOT A MAN TO TURN DOWN FREE MONEY, MISTER SAMPSON, BUT I'M NOT IN THE HABIT OF WASTING PEOPLE'S TIME *EITHER*.

I'VE SAILED THOSE WATERS MY ENTIRE LIFE AND I PROMISE YOU NOW THERE ARE NO ISLANDS IN THOSE PARTS FOR *A HUNDRED MILES*.

TRUST ME, BUDDY. IF *SHELDON* SAYS THERE'S AN ISLAND ON THAT SPOT YOU CAN PRETTY MUCH BET THE FARM ON IT.

OH *REALLY?* WHAT MAKES YOU SO *SURE?*

HE SAW IT IN A DREAM.

AND THE REST OF YOU ARE *COMFORTABLE* WITH THIS?

ENTIRELY COMFORTABLE.

ONE THING WE'VE LEARNED OVER THE YEARS IS THAT IF MY BROTHER GETS AN *IDEA* IN HIS HEAD THERE'S NO POINT TRYING TO TALK HIM *OUT* OF IT, CAPTAIN.

WELL, THERE'S NO DENYING YOU'RE A COLORFUL BUNCH AND YOU'VE CERTAINLY PIQUED MY *CURIOSITY* HERE. BUT IF I'M GOING TO COMMIT MY SHIP AND MY CREW I NEED A LITTLE MORE TO *GO* ON.

WHAT EXACTLY ARE YOU HOPING TO *FIND?*

TO TELL YOU THE TRUTH, I'M STILL NOT SURE. ALL I KNOW IS THAT THE COUNTRY I LOVE IS ON HER *KNEES* RIGHT NOW AND EVERYTHING I BELIEVE IN IS COMING APART AT THE SEAMS.

I LOST EVERYTHING I HAD IN THE CRASH OF '29, BUT I KNOW IN MY HEART THAT WE'RE GOING TO GET *THROUGH* THIS AND THE ANSWER TO EVERYTHING LIES ON THAT *ISLAND.*

AS WILD AS IT SOUNDS, IT'S BEEN *CALLING* ME THERE. BURNING LIKE A BEACON AND TELLING ME WHERE TO *FIND* IT.

I'VE TRAVELLED HALFWAY AROUND THE WORLD TO GET TO THIS POINT AND I'LL *SWIM* THE REST OF THE WAY IF I HAVE TO. SO WHAT DO YOU SAY, CAPTAIN? WILL YOU *HELP US OUT?*

SEE? I *TOLD* YOU HE WAS SERIOUS.

I'M EITHER *OUT OF MY MIND* OR VERY, VERY *DRUNK,* MISTER SAMPSON. BUT YOU'VE GOT YOURSELF A *SHIP.*

ALL MY LIFE I'D BEEN PRIVILEGED AND ASSURED. NOTHING HAD EVER GONE *WRONG* ON MY JOURNEY FROM SCHOOL TO YALE TO THE BOARD OF MY FATHER'S COMPANY.

THE WALL STREET CRASH WAS MY FIRST TASTE OF FAILURE AND THE EFFECT WAS *DEVASTATING*, BOTH PERSONALLY AND PROFESSIONALLY.

EVERYTHING WE HAD EVER EARNED WAS BLOWN AWAY IN A SINGLE DAY BY A PANIC ON THE NEW YORK STOCK EXCHANGE.

BUT MY OWN MISFORTUNE TROUBLED ME LESS THAN WHAT I SAW HAPPENING TO THE COUNTRY AT LARGE AS A RESULT OF THE PRESIDENT'S SUBSEQUENT *AUSTERITY DRIVE*.

AMERICA WAS THE GREATEST IDEA IN HUMAN HISTORY, THE MOST RESOURCEFUL PEOPLE THE WORLD HAD EVER KNOWN, AND YET HERE WE WERE REDUCED TO *BREADLINES* AND *SOUP KITCHENS*.

THE BOLSHEVIKS HAD ALREADY TAKEN RUSSIA AND THERE WERE RUMBLINGS OF REVOLUTION ALL ACROSS EUROPE.

MIGHT THE UNITED STATES BE NEXT TO FALL? COULD OUR ENTIRE FREE-MARKET INFRASTRUCTURE BE DESTROYED BY SOME *BAD LOANS* AND *RECKLESS BANKERS*?

THESE WERE THE THOUGHTS THAT WERE KEEPING ME AWAKE WHEN THE ISLAND FIRST *CALLED OUT* TO ME.

I COULD SEE IT IN MY DREAMS, LIKE LIBERTY'S TORCH, PROMISING SALVATION FOR A COUNTRY AND A CONSTITUTION THAT MEANT MORE TO ME THAN *LIFE ITSELF*.

OUR FINEST HOUR WAS *YET TO COME*, THE ISLAND ASSURED ME.

GREAT GIFTS LAY BENEATH ITS SHORES AND MY TASK WAS TO BRING THEM TO A NATION NEEDING *HEROES*.

MY UNCLE HAD ASKED ME TO JOIN THE BOARD OF A NEW VENTURE HE WAS PUTTING TOGETHER, BUT MY ONLY REAL INTEREST NOW WAS MAKING MY WAY TO *THE ISLAND.*

MY FIANCÉE TOLD EVERYONE I'D SUFFERED A COMPLETE MENTAL BREAKDOWN AND CALLED OFF OUR ENGAGEMENT, BUT NOTHING COULD KEEP ME FROM THAT DISTANT CALL.

I GATHERED MY BROTHER AND A FEW OLD COLLEGE BUDDIES AND BEGAN A JOURNEY THAT WOULD TAKE ME EAST THROUGH ENGLAND AND EUROPE AND EVENTUALLY NORTH AFRICA.

I WAS HUMBLED BY THEIR *BELIEF* IN ME. NEVER ONCE, IN ALL OUR MONTHS TOGETHER, DID THEY EVER BETRAY ONE SOLITARY DOUBT.

I GUESS IT'S EASIER TO *DRAW* THAN DESCRIBE, BUT THIS IS WHAT IT *LOOKS LIKE,* GUYS. THIS IS WHAT I SEE WHEN I CLOSE MY EYES.

THERE'S A HARBOR HERE ON THE *SOUTH* OF THE ISLAND AND THE REMAINS OF AN ANCIENT UNIVERSITY CAN BE ACCESSED THROUGH A CAVE UP HIGH ON THE *WESTERN SLOPES.*

THIS IS WHERE IT'S TELLING ME TO *BRING* THE CREW AND IT'S IN THESE WALLS WE'LL FIND THE KEY TO EVERYTHING I'VE BEEN *PROMISED.*

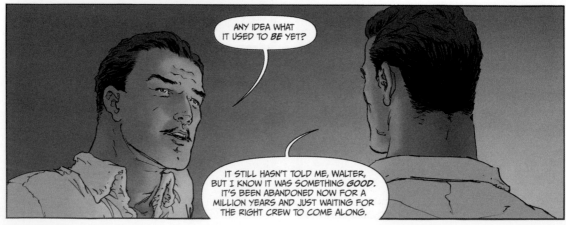

ANY IDEA WHAT IT USED TO *BE* YET?

IT STILL HASN'T TOLD ME, WALTER, BUT I KNOW IT WAS SOMETHING *GOOD.* IT'S BEEN ABANDONED NOW FOR A MILLION YEARS AND JUST WAITING FOR THE RIGHT CREW TO COME ALONG.

ARE YOU SURE MY CREW AND I ARE SUPPOSED *BE* HERE, MISTER SAMPSON?

THE ISLAND DOESN'T *MAKE* MISTAKES, CAPTAIN. YOU'RE HERE BECAUSE IT *WANTS* YOU TO BE HERE. WHO KNOWS? MAYBE IT SEES SOMETHING IN YOU THAT YOU CAN'T SEE FOR *YOURSELF.*

WE'VE NEVER *TALKED* ABOUT WHAT HAPPENED IN THOSE MOUNTAINS. ALL PEOPLE KNOW IS THAT WE CAME BACK BETTER AND WRAPPED IN COSTUMES THAT RAISED THE SPIRITS OF ANYONE WHO *SAW* THEM.

THE PAPERS CALLED US *SUPERHEROES* AND WE HELPED AMERICA THROUGH THE GREAT DEPRESSION, THE SECOND WORLD WAR, CONFLICTS, SCANDALS AND ANYTHING THAT WAS *THROWN* AT US.

WE DIDN'T CARE ABOUT MONEY OR POLITICS. OUR ONLY DESIRE WAS TO *SERVE OUR COUNTRY* AND OUR INFINITE IDEALISM INSPIRED THE BEST IN EVERYONE WHO CAME *NEAR* US.

...AND SO WE HAD CHILDREN TO CARRY ON OUR WORK AND INSPIRE OUR GREAT NATION TO *EVEN MORE* REMARKABLE HEIGHTS.

SUPERHEROES WERE THE SUMMIT OF *AMERICAN ASPIRATION* AND SO OUR CHILDREN GREW UP TO REMIND MANKIND OF EVERYTHING WE COULD EVER HOPE TO BE.

LOOK AT HER. SHE WILL LITERALLY PUT HER NAME ON *ANYTHING*, WON'T SHE? SHE DOESN'T GIVE A *DAMN* ABOUT ENDOMETRIOSIS. CHLOE COULDN'T EVEN *SPELL* ENDOMETRIOSIS.

SHE'S JUST TRYING TO SUCK UP TO YOUR *PARENTS*, MAN. SHE KNOWS LADY LIBERTY LOVES A GOOD *CHARITABLE FOUNDATION*.

OH, THIS IS BIGGER THAN HER AND MOM, DUDE. BELIEVE ME, THIS IS ALL ABOUT HER *ENDORSEMENTS*.

THE MORE OF *THESE* SHE DOES EVERY WEEK THE MORE BIG BRANDS WILL WANT TO BE *ASSOCIATED* WITH HER. AM I THE ONLY ONE WHO CAN SEE HOW *CYNICAL* SHE IS?

UH, EXCUSE ME? ARE YOU BRANDON SAMPSON? I JUST WANTED TO LET YOU KNOW THAT YOUR PARENTS WERE MY BIGGEST *INFLUENCE*.

I WOULDN'T EVEN BE *WEARING* THIS COSTUME IF IT WASN'T FOR ALL THE AMAZING WORK THEY'VE DONE OVER THE YEARS.

YEAH, WELL. THAT'S VERY INTERESTING, SWEETHEART, BUT THIS IS THE *VIP* AREA AND YOU'RE NOT ALLOWED TO CROSS THAT LINE UNLESS YOU'VE GOT *SUPER-POWERS*.

ACTUALLY, MY FRIEND AND I WERE WONDERING IF YOU COULD MAYBE HELP GET US *IN*. WE JUST MOVED HERE FROM SALT LAKE CITY AND STILL ON THE LOOK-OUT FOR A PUBLICIST AND AN AGENT.

OH, MAN. HERE WE GO....

IF YOU'RE AFTER WHAT I *THINK* YOU'RE AFTER JUST WAIT FOR ME IN THE *MEN'S ROOM*, HONEY. I'LL BE FINISHED WITH THESE DRINKS IN *FIVE MINUTES*, BUT I'M NOT TAKING MY *CLOTHES* OFF. UNDERSTAND?

OH MY GOD. WHAT MAKES YOU THINK YOU CAN *TALK* TO PEOPLE LIKE THAT?

YOU THINK BECAUSE YOUR DAD'S THE UTOPIAN YOU'RE *BETTER* THAN EVERYONE ELSE?

LEAVE IT, KENDRA. THE GUY'S AN *IDIOT.* LET'S GO TALK TO SOMEBODY ELSE.

YOUR LOSS, LADIES

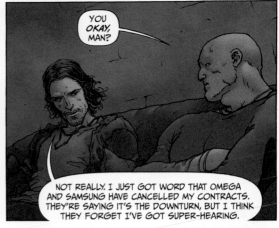

YOU *OKAY,* MAN?

NOT REALLY. I JUST GOT WORD THAT OMEGA AND SAMSUNG HAVE CANCELLED MY CONTRACTS. THEY'RE SAYING IT'S THE DOWNTURN, BUT I THINK THEY FORGET I'VE GOT SUPER-HEARING.

YOU JUST NEED TO RAISE YOUR *PROFILE,* DUDE. GET OUT THERE AGAIN AND MAYBE *SAVE* SOME PEOPLE. IT'S THE ONLY WAY TO GET YOUR FACE *VIRAL.*

DOING WHAT? MY DAD'S ALWAYS *TELLING* ME I NEED TO DO MORE SUPERHERO STUFF, BUT THIS ISN'T LIKE THE OLD DAYS. THERE'S NOBODY COOL TO *FIGHT* ANYMORE.

ALL THE GREAT BATTLES ARE WELL AND TRULY *OVER.* ALL THE BEST VILLAINS DIED *TEN* OR *TWENTY* YEARS AGO. MY PARENTS NEED TO REALIZE THEY WERE LIVING IN A *GOLDEN AGE.*

UH, *EXCUSE* ME?

I DON'T MEAN TO INTERRUPT, BUT MY FRIEND ASKED ME TO LET YOU KNOW SHE'S WAITING IN *THE MEN'S ROOM* WHEN YOU'RE READY.

VERMONT:

HEY, JULES. WHAT'S *GOING ON?* I JUST GOT THE TEXT. IS THIS REALLY *BLACKSTAR* EVERYBODY'S FIGHTING UP THERE?

YEAH, THAT'S WHY I'M HANGING BACK AND WAITING TO SEE WHAT *HAPPENS.* A HUNDRED DIFFERENT HEROES SHOWED UP, BUT *I'M* NOT GOING UP AGAINST A GUY WITH AN ANTI-MATTER BATTERY IN HIS CHEST.

ISN'T HE THE ONE THAT KILLED THAT ENTIRE *ALIEN RACE?*

TELL ME ABOUT IT. I'LL JUMP IN AT THE END AND LAND A FEW BLOWS, BUT IN THE MEANTIME I'M JUST MOVING AROUND AND DOING MY BEST TO AVOID GETTING *HIT.*

MY DAD AND UNCLE SHELDON'S UP FRONT *ANYWAY* SO IT'S NOT LIKE THERE'S ANYTHING TO *WORRY* ABOUT.

SPEAKING OF WHICH, I HEARD YOU GOT BUMPED FROM THE MAIN TEAM AGAIN AT THE *MEETING* THIS AFTERNOON. WHAT THE HELL'S UP WITH *THAT?*

AH, YOU KNOW WHAT MY *UNCLE'S* LIKE. HE STILL HASN'T FORGIVEN ME FOR GOING ON A DATE WITH THAT WOMAN I RESCUED FROM A *HOUSE FIRE* LAST YEAR.

HE ACTUALLY SAID I WAS *MORALLY QUESTIONABLE,* BUT *HE'S* THE ONE WHO'S MORALS I'D *QUESTION.* GUY'S STILL LIVING IN *1935.*

OH NO.

WHAT'S UP?

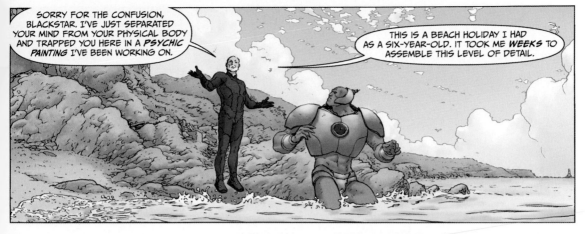

W-WOW.

NOT EXACTLY THE *NOBLEST* WAY WE'VE EVER WON A FIGHT, BUT, I HOPE, FORGIVABLE UNDER THE CIRCUMSTANCES. IS EVERYONE OKAY?

JUST A LITTLE *WINDED*, UTOPIAN. DOES ANYONE HAVE A BOTTLE OF *WATER?*

BLACKSTAR LEVELED *HALF OF MISSOURI* THE LAST TIME HE ESCAPED FROM THE GOVERNMENT'S *HOLDING PEN.* AT LEAST WE TOOK HIM DOWN WITHOUT ANY *CASUALTIES* THIS TIME.

JUST NOTIFYING THE SUPERMAX *RIGHT NOW,* SIR. I'LL TELL THEM WE'LL BE ABOUT *TWENTY MINUTES* IF THE WIND ISN'T AGAINST US.

HEY, UNCLE SHELDON. WHO'S HANDLING *FIRST AID* TONIGHT? I REALLY GOT *WINDED* BACK THERE AND I THINK I MIGHT HAVE CUT MY *KNEE.*

OH, DON'T EVEN *TRY* TO PRETEND YOU WERE INVOLVED IN THIS, JULES. I *HEARD* YOU ON THE PHONE TO YOUR PUBLICIST. DOES BEING IN THE PAPERS REALLY MATTER *THAT MUCH* TO YOU?

AT LEAST WALTER'S BOY *SHOWED UP,* HONEY.

STILL NO WORD FROM THE KIDS?

NOT EVEN A REPLY. BUT THAT'S HARDLY A SHOCK. IT'S GOTTEN TO THE POINT I'D BE MORE SURPRISED IF THEY *DID* RESPOND TO AN EMERGENCY CALL.

I THINK THAT'S A LITTLE *UNFAIR,* GRACE.

EXCUSE ME?

YOU HAVE TO REMEMBER THEY DIDN'T *CHOOSE* THIS LIFE. THEY WERE *BORN* INTO THE FAMILY BUSINESS.

YOU CAN'T GIVE THEM A HARD TIME BECAUSE THEY'D RATHER GO TO A MOVIE PREMIERE THAN TAKE PART IN A STREET FIGHT.

WELL, I THINK WE'D *ALL* RATHER BE AT A PARTY RIGHT NOW, BUT HAVING THESE POWERS COMES WITH CERTAIN *RESPONSIBILITIES.*

EXCUSE ME WHILE I BITE MY TONGUE.

WHAT DO YOU MEAN BY THAT?

GENTLEMEN, PLEASE. LET'S NOT *GET INTO* ALL THIS AGAIN...

NO, *LET'S.* AMERICA'S *COLLAPSING,* THE EURO-ZONE'S *BLEEDING TO DEATH,* THE GLOBAL ECONOMY'S HANGING BY A *THREAD* AND WE'RE STILL JUST OUT THERE *WRESTLING* LIKE *CHILDREN.*

DON'T YOU THINK WE COULD HELP MORE *DIRECTLY?* DOESN'T THIS GIVE YOU A HORRIFIC SENSE OF IMPOTENCE?

YOU'RE NOT AN *ECONOMIST,* WALTER. WHAT ARE YOU GOING TO DO? JUST BECAUSE YOU CAN FLY DOESN'T MEAN YOU KNOW HOW TO BALANCE A *BUDGET.*

YOU NEED TO ACCEPT THAT WE'RE *PUBLIC SERVANTS* AND HAVE A LITTLE FAITH IN THE GOVERNMENT WE'VE *ELECTED.*

OH, MY DEAR, SWEET BROTHER. IT'S THE POLITICIANS WHO ARE MESSING IT UP. DON'T YOU UNDERSTAND? PEOPLE ARE *PLEADING* FOR SOMEONE TO STEP IN AND FIX THIS CHAOS.

I KNOW YOU THINK MAN ALWAYS FINDS A WAY, BUT WE'RE RIGHT BACK WHERE WE WERE IN 1929. THIS AMERICA WE'RE SUPPOSED TO PROTECT IS ALMOST ON THE VERGE OF BEING *WASHED AWAY.*

I'M SURE THE PRESIDENT KNOWS WHAT HE'S DOING, WALTER. HE DOESN'T NEED US TO TELL HIM HOW TO RUN THE COUNTRY.

OH, OF COURSE. BECAUSE THEY'RE SO MUCH SMARTER THAN WE ARE. THAT'S WHY THEY LET THE BANKS RUN WILD LIKE THEY DID IN '29 AND STARTED ALL THOSE *WARS* WE COULDN'T AFFORD.

I SAW A FOOD LINE IN *LOS ANGELES* THIS MORNING, GRACE. HOW BAD DOES IT HAVE TO GET BEFORE WE FINALLY ADMIT THAT THE SYSTEM *DOESN'T WORK* ANYMORE?

4 AM, LOS ANGELES:

WAS SHE *MAD* AT YOU?

TO BE HONEST, MOM'S ALWAYS KIND OF MAD AT ME. I TRIED TO EXPLAIN THAT MY CELL PHONE WAS OFF, BUT SHE HATES THE FACT THAT I'M SO *NONCONFRONTATIONAL.*

I THOUGHT SHE'D BE *PLEASED* ABOUT MY CHARITY FOUNDATION, BUT ALL SHE WANTS IS ME *PUNCHING PEOPLE IN THE FACE.*

ECONOMIC DOWNTURN

HOW CAN I HURT ANOTHER LIVING BEING? I'M A BUDDHIST AND A VEGETARIAN. I'M NOT GOING TO HURT SOMEONE BECAUSE THEY CONTRADICT OUR *BELIEF SYSTEM.*

OH, POOR, LITTLE *RICH GIRL.* COME AND MAKE IT ALL GO AWAY WITH LIONEL'S MAGIC NOSE POWDER.

WE GOT THIS STUFF FROM AN OFF-WORLD DEALER, CHLOE. YOU'LL *LOVE* IT. I'M MORE MESSED UP THAN THAT TIME WE DROPPED ACID IN THE MARIANAS TRENCH.

FINANCIAL CRISIS DEEPENING

EVERYONE THINKS IT MUST BE GREAT WHEN YOUR PARENTS ARE FAMOUS SUPERHEROES, BUT THEY REALLY HAVE *NO IDEA.*

I'LL NEVER BE AS COOL AS DAD OR AS BEAUTIFUL AS MOM. LOOK AT ME: I'M LIKE THE WORST ASPECTS OF BOTH OF THEM. I EVEN HAVE UGLY FEET .

OH, DARLING. GET OVER YOURSELF.

WIDESPREAD UNEMPLOYMENT

I'M *SERIOUS*. MY MOM'S LIKE A HUNDRED YEARS OLD AND GUYS STILL ONLY HIT ON ME TO SEE IF THEY CAN GET HER PHONE NUMBER.

MORAL DECLINE...

SPEAKING OF WHICH, WHAT'S GOING ON WITH YOU AND *SHOCKWAVE*? I SAW YOU TALKING TO HIM FOR LIKE, AN HOUR OUTSIDE THE LITTLE GIRLS' ROOM EARLIER.

EW, NOT A CHANCE. DATING A SUPERHERO WOULD BE LIKE DATING MY FATHER. I'LL STICK WITH DISAPPOINTING *BAD BOYS* IF YOU DON'T MIND.

YOU KNOW MY PARENTS HAVE NEVER SAID A MEAN WORD IN ALL THOSE *YEARS* THEY'VE BEEN TOGETHER? THEY'RE BOTH JUST SO *BEAUTIFUL* AND *UNCOMPLICATED*.

ALL THEY WANT IS TO *LOVE EACH OTHER* AND *HELP OTHER PEOPLE*. YOU KNOW THEY'RE THE LAST TWO HEROES WHO STILL KEEP *SECRET IDS*?

MY THERAPIST SAID THAT'S WHY I NEVER MAINTAIN A PROPER RELATIONSHIP. I'M ALWAYS COMPARING IT TO THIS PERFECT THING I SAW *GROWING UP*.

COVERT OPERATION

I...

CHLOE, ARE YOU *OKAY*?

COMING UP...

YEAH, IT'S JUST... WOW. THIS IS REALLY *STRONG STUFF*. I MEAN...

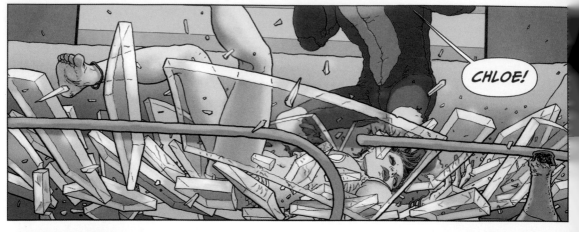

CHAPTER 2

THE BAY AREA:

DAD'S GOING TO *LOVE* THIS. THIS IS EXACTLY THE KIND OF THING HE'S ALWAYS *TELLING* ME *I* SHOULD BE DOING.

HE SAYS WHEN I DON'T HAVE *SUPERVILLAINS* TO FIGHT I SHOULD BE OUT THERE DRUMMING UP BUSINESS AND *LOOKING* FOR WAYS TO HELP PEOPLE.

WELL, IT DOESN'T GET MUCH MORE AWESOME THAN *THIS*, HUH?

ABSOLUTELY.

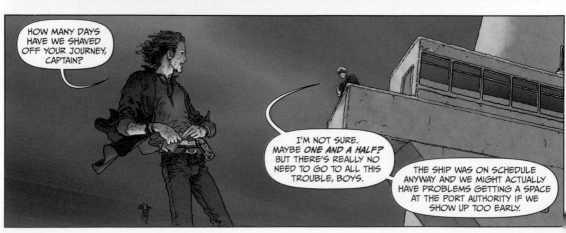

HOW MANY DAYS HAVE WE SHAVED OFF YOUR JOURNEY, CAPTAIN?

I'M NOT SURE. MAYBE *ONE AND A HALF?* BUT THERE'S REALLY NO NEED TO GO TO ALL THIS TROUBLE, BOYS.

THE SHIP WAS ON SCHEDULE ANYWAY AND WE MIGHT ACTUALLY HAVE PROBLEMS GETTING A SPACE AT THE PORT AUTHORITY IF WE SHOW UP TOO EARLY.

NO TROUBLE *AT ALL*, SIR. OUR *PLEASURE*. JUST TELL THE CREW TO SIT BACK AND RELAX AND WE'LL HAVE YOU IN SAN DIEGO IN A LITTLE OVER TWO HOURS.

MAN, I STILL CAN'T BELIEVE HOW MUCH WE *PUT AWAY* BACK THERE. I MUST HAVE HAD ABOUT FIFTY SHOTS.

HOW MUCH DID YOU DRINK, BRANDON? I SAW YOU HAVE TWENTY WITH THAT KENDRA GIRL, BUT YOU MUST HAVE DONE ANOTHER FIFTY WHEN WE GOT TO THE ROXY.

DUDE, WOULD YOU *SHUT UP?* I CAN'T COUNT AND DO TELEKINESIS AT THE SAME TIME. YOU'RE TOTALLY PUTTING ME OFF.

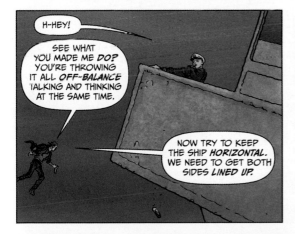

H-HEY!

SEE WHAT YOU MADE ME *DO?* YOU'RE THROWING IT ALL *OFF-BALANCE* TALKING AND THINKING AT THE SAME TIME.

NOW TRY TO KEEP THE SHIP *HORIZONTAL*. WE NEED TO GET BOTH SIDES *LINED UP*.

SHIT!

GET OUT OF THE *WAY!*

WHAT ARE YOU *DOING?* YOU'RE *FLIPPING* IT!

WHAT?

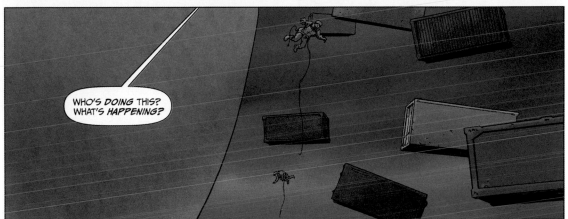

DAD! THANK GOD!

SHUT UP, BRANDON. DO YOU REALIZE HOW MANY PEOPLE COULD HAVE BEEN *KILLED* BACK THERE? DO YOU UNDERSTAND WHAT WOULD HAVE HAPPENED IF I HADN'T BEEN *ON PATROL?*

RELAX, DUDE. WE WERE TOTALLY, TOTALLY *ON IT.*

NO, YOU'RE SO DRUNK YOU CAN BARELY STRING A *SENTENCE* TOGETHER. IT'S BAD ENOUGH YOU DON'T *ATTEND* EMERGENCIES WITHOUT GETTING OUT OF YOUR MIND AND *CAUSING* THEM.

I EXPECTED MORE FROM *YOU,* SHOCKWAVE. YOUR GRANDPARENTS WOULD BE *APPALLED* IF THEY WERE ALIVE TO SEE THIS.

OH, *SCREW YOU,* DAD! DON'T ACT LIKE YOU EXPECTED IT FROM *ME!*

WHAT THE HELL'S YOUR PROBLEM *ANYWAY?* YOU'RE ANGRY WHEN *I DON'T* PLAY SUPERHERO AND YOU'RE ANGRY WHEN WHEN *I DO.*

MY *PROBLEM* IS THAT I WANTED A *SUCCESSOR* AND ENDED UP WITH A *DISGRACE!*

I'M *ASHAMED* OF YOUR BEHAVIOR! *DISGUSTED* BY THIS SHALLOW CELEBRITY YOU SEEM TO HAVE *CHOSEN* FOR YOURSELF!

NOW GET DOWN THERE AND WAIT BEHIND THE SHOPPING MALL ON THE NORTH EAST SIDE OF THE CITY. I'LL HAVE YOUR MOTHER STOP BY AND PICK EVERYONE UP WHEN SHE GETS A MOMENT!

UH, I THINK WE'RE CAPABLE OF GETTING *OURSELVES* HOME, MAN.

LOS ANGELES:

emergency

CHLOE? CAN YOU *HEAR* ME? IT'S DOCTOR OBERMAN. I'M AFRAID YOU'VE HAD ANOTHER *OVERDOSE.*

WH-WHAT?

YOUR FRIENDS FLEW YOU HERE AT 4 A.M. LAST NIGHT AND SAID YOU'D INGESTED AN *ALIEN SUBSTANCE.*

YOUR HEART STOPPED *WORKING* FOR TEN OR ELEVEN MINUTES, BUT YOUR MOTHER HELPED ME GET A NEEDLE THROUGH YOUR CHEST AND WE MANAGED TO GET IT BEATING AGAIN.

MY *M-MOM* KNOWS ABOUT THIS?

EVERYBODY KNOWS, I'M AFRAID. WE'VE GOT HALF THE WORLD'S MEDIA OUT THERE TRYING TO GET A PAPARAZZI SPECIAL THROUGH THE CURTAINS.

BUT YOU'RE GOING TO BE FINE AND *THE BABY'S* FINE TOO. WE DID AN *ULTRASOUND* WHEN YOU WERE STILL OUT COLD AND THE OBSTETRICIAN SAID YOU'RE BOTH DOING WELL.

BOTH?

WHAT ARE YOU *TALKING* ABOUT?

AH.

I'M SORRY. I THOUGHT YOU *KNEW.*

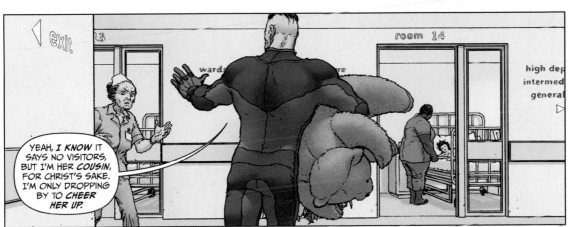

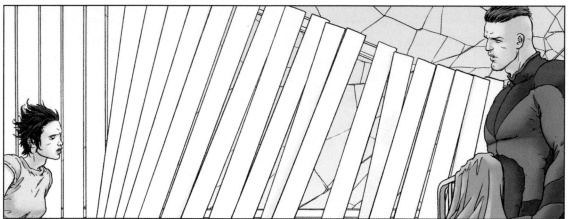

WELL, SCREW YOU.

IT'S OKAY, IT'S OKAY. WE'VE GOT PEOPLE HERE IF YOU NEED TO *TALK IT OVER.* YOU'RE NOT THE FIRST GIRL TO COME IN HERE AND GET *BLIND-SIDED* LIKE THIS. IS THERE A *FATHER* ON THE SCENE?

KIND OF.

IS IT *COMPLICATED?*

VERY.

LONG BEACH:

Kebabe

the BLARNEY inn
caed mile failte

WELL, WELL, WELL. IF IT ISN'T MY OLD FRIEND *HUTCH*.

NOT SO FAST, BUD. *I'LL* TAKE THE POWER ROD IF YOU DON'T MIND.

WE *HEARD* YOU WERE BACK IN TOWN, BUT WE DIDN'T THINK YOU'D BE STUPID ENOUGH TO HANG AROUND YOUR OLD *WATERING HOLE*.

YOU FORGET YOU OWE THE BIG MAN FOR THAT SUITCASE FULL OF *HEROIN* THAT WENT WALKIES LAST CHRISTMAS?

'COURSE I DIDN'T FORGET. HOW DO YOU THINK I PAID FOR ALL THIS BOOZE.

THE BIG MAN PUT A HUNDRED "G"S ON THAT SMART MOUTH, HUTCH. THAT'S FIFTY GRAND EACH FOR ME AND MY BROTHER IF WE HAUL YOUR ASS DOWN TO *THE CLUB*.

NOW DON'T TRY ANYTHING *FOOLISH*. YOU'RE ONLY GONNA MAKE IT WORSE. WE'VE GOT *STRENGTH, SPEED, SONIC SCREAMS* AND *OPTIC BLASTS*...

...NOT TO MENTION THIS LITTLE *POWER ROD* YOU'RE ALWAYS WAVING AROUND. WHAT YOU GOTTA SAY TO *THAT*?

SHARK-INFESTED WATERS.

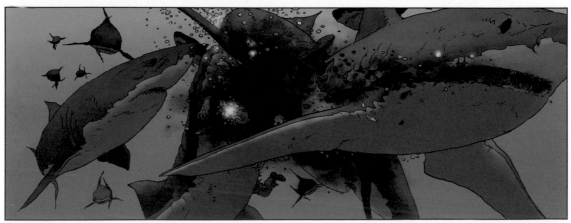

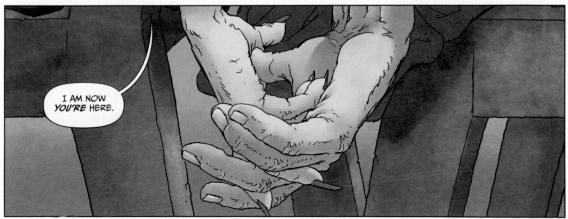

SANTA MONICA:

YOU KNOW THE *WORST* THING ABOUT A DRUG OVERDOSE? THE *EMBARRASSMENT FACTOR*...

EVERYONE ASSUMES YOU TRIED TO *COMMIT SUICIDE*. LIKE MY PAMPERED LIFE IS SO DAMN STRESSFUL THAT I COULDN'T EVEN COPE WITH A CHARITY-BALL. I HATE IT WHEN PEOPLE THINK I'M VACUOUS..

THE WORST THING FOR ME WAS NOT BEING ABLE TO *SEE* YOU. THAT'S THE ONLY THING I DON'T LIKE ABOUT OUR THING. THE FACT WE NEED TO KEEP IT *HIDDEN*.

WELL, IT'S NOT GOING TO GET ANY *EASIER*. DID YOU HEAR MY ADDICTION COUNSELLOR HAS ARRANGED FOR ME TO MOVE BACK IN WITH MY *PARENTS* FOR THREE MONTHS?

THAT'S THREE MORE MONTHS IN MY ALTER-EGO, BUMPING INTO FURNITURE AND PRETENDING I'M A GEEK AGAIN.

CAN'T YOU JUST SAY NO?

NOT IF I WANT TO HANG ONTO MY *ADVERTISING CONTRACTS*.

BESIDES, IF YOU EVER ACTUALLY MEET MY MOM YOU'LL REALIZE SHE'S NOT EXACTLY SOMEONE PEOPLE LIKE SAYING *NO* TO.

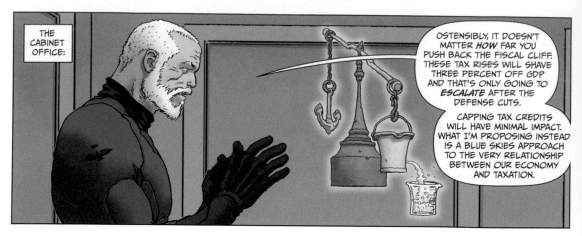

THE CABINET OFFICE:

OSTENSIBLY, IT DOESN'T MATTER *HOW* FAR YOU PUSH BACK THE FISCAL CLIFF. THESE TAX RISES WILL SHAVE THREE PERCENT OFF GDP AND THAT'S ONLY GOING TO *ESCALATE* AFTER THE DEFENSE CUTS.

CAPPING TAX CREDITS WILL HAVE MINIMAL IMPACT. WHAT I'M PROPOSING INSTEAD IS A BLUE SKIES APPROACH TO THE VERY RELATIONSHIP BETWEEN OUR ECONOMY AND TAXATION.

AT EASE, GENTLEMEN.

WALTER, I'D LIKE A *WORD*.

NOT NOW, UTOPIAN. I'M IN THE MIDDLE OF A *MEETING*.

I SAID A *WORD*, PLEASE, WALTER.

FORGIVE ME, LADIES AND GENTLEMEN, BUT I'M AFRAID THIS IS THE ONE PERSON MY PSYCHIC POWERS *DON'T WORK* ON.

NO, BECAUSE YOU'RE NOT AS SMART AS YOU *THINK* YOU ARE.

YOU'RE MY BROTHER AND I LOVE YOU, BUT YOU'VE ALWAYS BEEN DRIVEN BY *RELENTLESS EGO* AND I REFUSE TO LET YOU SCARE THEM INTO HANDING YOU *CONTROL*.

THE SYSTEM *WORKS*. WE JUST HAVE TO *TRUST* IT. NOW GO BACK AND TELL THE PRESIDENT THIS IS ALL VERY FLATTERING, BUT IT'S NOT OUR JOB TO TELL *GOVERNMENTS* WHAT TO DO.

WHY *NOT*?

BECAUSE I *SAID* SO.

AND YOU WONDER WHY YOUR CHILDREN ARE A DISENFRANCHISED *MESS*?

JUST GET IN THERE AND DO AS YOU'RE *TOLD*.

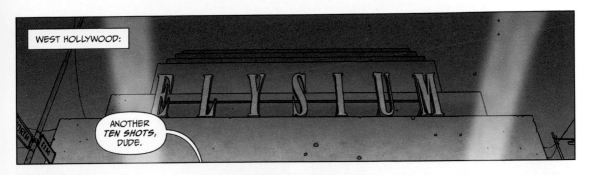

WEST HOLLYWOOD:

ELYSIUM

ANOTHER *TEN SHOTS*, DUDE.

IN FACT, MAKE IT ANOTHER *TWENTY*. IT'LL SAVE ME *CATCHING YOUR EYE* AGAIN IN FIVE MINUTES.

I HEARD ABOUT WHAT HAPPENED, BRANDON. THE BOYS WERE SAYING HE *HUMILIATED* YOU AGAIN AND I JUST WANTED TO CHECK YOU WERE DOING *OKAY*.

YEAH, WELL. LET'S JUST SAY I'M *GETTING USED* TO IT, UNCLE WALTER.

I JUST WISH HE'D STOP *COMPARING* US. IT'S SO *UNFAIR*. I *KNOW* I'M NOT AS SMART AS HE IS. I *KNOW* I'LL NEVER BE THE SAME *PERFECT EXAMPLE* OF *AMERICAN MASCULINITY*.

OH, YOUR FATHER ISN'T *PERFECT*, BRANDON. BELIEVE ME. YOU HAVE TO REMEMBER I WAS *THERE* BACK IN THE OLD DAYS

IT'S *ONLY HUMAN* TO IDEALIZE OUR PARENTS, BUT THE OLD HAVE REALLY NO MORE WISDOM THAN *THE YOUNG*. WE'RE JUST UGLY ENOUGH TO *LOOK* WISE AND NOT SO DRIVEN BY OUR *GENITALIA*.

I *HATE* HIM, MAN. I TOTALLY *HATE* HIM. I KNOW HE'S MY DAD AND I'M SUPPOSED TO LOVE HIM, BUT I REALLY WANT TO *STRANGLE* HIM WHEN HE MAKES ME FEEL THIS LOW.

SO DO SOMETHING *ABOUT* IT.

WHAT?

YOU'RE NOT THE *ONLY* ONE HE'S ALIENATED WITH THAT HIGH-HANDED ATTITUDE. I'VE HAD *DECADES* OF THAT ARROGANT ASS AND HE TALKS TO MY BOY LIKE SOME VULGAR *C-LISTER.*

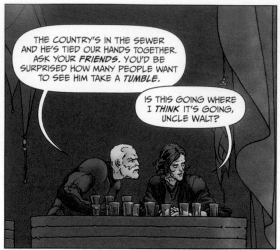

THE COUNTRY'S IN THE SEWER AND HE'S TIED OUR HANDS TOGETHER. ASK YOUR *FRIENDS.* YOU'D BE SURPRISED HOW MANY PEOPLE WANT TO SEE HIM TAKE A *TUMBLE.*

IS THIS GOING WHERE I *THINK* IT'S GOING, UNCLE WALT?

YOU KNOW YOU'RE VERY WELL-REGARDED IN *THE COMMUNITY,* BRANDON, SO LET ME ASK YOU A *HYPOTHETICAL QUESTION...*

...IF YOUR FATHER WERE TO FALL UNDER A BUS WOULD YOU HAVE THE COURAGE TO REALLY DO WHAT NEEDS TO BE DONE OUT THERE?

ARE YOU *SERIOUS?*

I'VE SPOKEN TO A LOT OF *PEOPLE* LATELY AND YOURS IS THE NAME THAT KEEPS *COMING UP.*

IT'S OBVIOUS YOU'RE THE ONLY ONE WHO COULD CHALLENGE HIM *PHYSICALLY,* BUT WHAT DO YOU THINK? IS LEADING SOMETHING THAT *APPEALS* IN ANY WAY?

ABSOLUTELY.

CHAPTER 3

LOS ANGELES:

UH, EXCUSE ME. I'M LOOKING FOR *THE UTOPIAN?*

WOULD YOU KEEP YOUR *VOICE* DOWN, PLEASE? THERE'RE *CIVILIANS* AROUND. THE NAME'S SHELDON SAMPSON WHEN I'M WEARING MY GLASSES. NEVER USE A CODENAME WHEN A MAN'S IN HIS SECRET IDENTITY.

YEAH, WHAT'S *WITH* ALL THIS, DUDE? YOU'RE THE BIGGEST SUPERHERO ON THE *PLANET.* WHY ARE YOU *FIXING CARBURETORS?*

NO SHAME IN AN *HONEST DAY'S WORK.* A SECRET IDENTITY HELPS KEEP YOU GROUNDED. IT'S IMPORTANT TO REMEMBER HOW THE PEOPLE WE *SERVE* LIVE THEIR LIVES.

UH, RIGHT. WELL, I GOT A TEXT SAYING YOU WANTED TO *MEET UP.* HOW DID YOU EVEN GET MY *NUMBER?*

I'M *THE UTOPIAN,* HUTCH. I KNOW *EVERYONE'S* NUMBER.

NOW COME INSIDE AND LET'S GRAB A *COFFEE.* THERE'S SOMETHING WE NEED TO DISCUSS.

DID THE PRESIDENT REALLY ASK FOR ME SPECIFICALLY, UNCLE WALTER?

WHY *WOULDN'T* HE? YOU'RE THE *LOGICAL CHOICE*, BRANDON. WITH YOUR *PARENTS* OUT OF THE WAY, YOU COULD USE YOUR POWERS TO PULL US OUT OF THIS HORRIBLE *RECESSION*.

OF COURSE, THEY WANT YOU TO FOLLOW MY *BASIC BLUEPRINTS*, BUT THE POLITICIANS ARE AS SCARED AS *EVERYBODY* ELSE RIGHT NOW.

I READ YOUR RENEWAL PLAN LAST NIGHT AND IT *BLEW MY MIND.*

CLIMATE ENGINEERING, ELIMINATING INCOME TAX, UNDERGROUND HOMES, A BAN ON ALL RELIGIONS. I COULD HARDLY *SLEEP* MY HEAD WAS SO BUZZING.

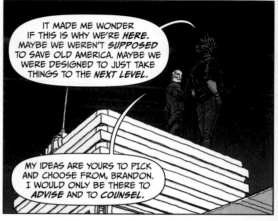

IT MADE ME WONDER IF THIS IS WHY WE'RE *HERE.* MAYBE WE WEREN'T *SUPPOSED* TO SAVE OLD AMERICA. MAYBE WE WERE DESIGNED TO JUST TAKE THINGS TO THE *NEXT LEVEL.*

MY IDEAS ARE YOURS TO PICK AND CHOOSE FROM, BRANDON. I WOULD ONLY BE THERE TO *ADVISE* AND TO *COUNSEL.*

NOW ARE YOU SURE YOU'RE PREPARED FOR THE *BIG CONFRONTATION?*

I CAN HANDLE YOUR MOTHER AND SISTER, BUT YOUR FATHER IS *ANOTHER* MATTER. ARE YOU SURE YOU'RE READY TO GO *HEAD-TO-HEAD* WITH HIM AT LAST?

TOTALLY.

GOOD.

BUT REMEMBER TO WAIT FOR THAT *PERFECT MOMENT.* THE OTHERS WILL *SOFTEN HIM UP* FOR YOU FIRST.

I WANT YOU TO STAY AWAY FROM MY *DAUGHTER.* DO YOU UNDERSTAND? THIS RELATIONSHIP WITH CHLOE ENDS *NOW.*

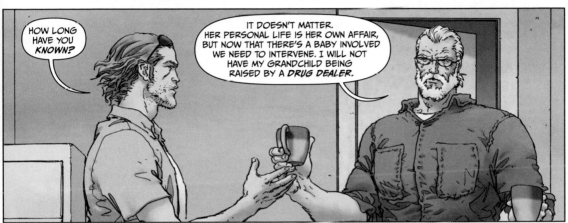

HOW LONG HAVE YOU *KNOWN?*

IT DOESN'T MATTER. HER PERSONAL LIFE IS HER OWN AFFAIR, BUT NOW THAT THERE'S A BABY INVOLVED WE NEED TO INTERVENE. I WILL NOT HAVE MY GRANDCHILD BEING RAISED BY A *DRUG DEALER.*

DRUG *DISTRIBUTOR,* SIR. TOTALLY DIFFERENT INCOME BRACKET.

IF THAT'S SUPPOSED TO BE A JOKE, I DON'T APPRECIATE YOUR SENSE OF HUMOR, MISTER HUTCHENCE.

NOW MY WIFE AND I WILL SUPPORT OUR DAUGHTER ANY WAY WE CAN. WE'VE EVEN OFFERED TO *ADOPT* THE BABY, BUT IF SHE'S REALLY GOING TO GET BACK ON HER FEET SHE NEEDS YOU OUT OF HER LIFE ENTIRELY.

WHAT IF I TOLD YOU I WAS PLANNING TO GO *STRAIGHT?* THAT I WAS SO IN LOVE WITH THIS GIRL THAT I'M WILLING TO *SETTLE DOWN* AND *CHANGE MY WAYS?*

LIKE YOUR FATHER?

ENCINO :

I CAN'T BELIEVE I'M ACTUALLY *LIVING HERE* AGAIN.

WELL, I'M SORRY IT'S NOT A *MANSION*, CHLOE, BUT I'M AFRAID WE CAN'T ALL HAVE THOSE BIG MILLION-DOLLAR *ADVERTISING CONTRACTS*.

OH, I DIDN'T MEAN THAT. YOUR HOUSE IS *REALLY NICE*, MOM. I JUST MEAN BACK IN MY SECRET IDENTITY AND SLEEPING IN MY OLD BEDROOM. IT'S THAT TOTAL SENSE OF *FAILURE*. LIKE I CAN'T CUT ADULT LIFE.

YOU GREW UP WITH PRESSURES WE'RE ONLY BEGINNING TO UNDERSTAND, DARLING. YOUR ADDICTIONS ARE JUST YOUR COPING MECHANISM AND I'M SORRY IF WE HAVEN'T *APPRECIATED* THAT ENOUGH.

HOW ARE YOU *FEELING*?

A LITTLE *PUKEY*, TO BE HONEST. I'VE ACTUALLY BEEN VOMITING EVERY MORNING FOR THE PAST TWO MONTHS, BUT I THOUGHT IT WAS JUST MY USUAL *HANGOVERS*.

I'VE REALLY SCREWED THINGS UP, HUH? YOU AND DAD MUST BE TOTALLY *ASHAMED*.

NOT IN THE *SLIGHTEST. WE'RE* THE ONES WHO SHOULD BE ASHAMED FOR NOT *BEING AROUND* ENOUGH.

BUDGE DEFENSE CUTS

STORMS COMING... NO

YOUR FATHER IS ACTUALLY VERY *EXCITED* ABOUT THIS PREGNANCY. HE DUG OUT ALL YOUR OLD TOYS AND WAS CLEANING THEM UP BEFORE HE CAME TO *BED* LAST NIGHT. IT WAS REALLY, VERY SWEET. I...

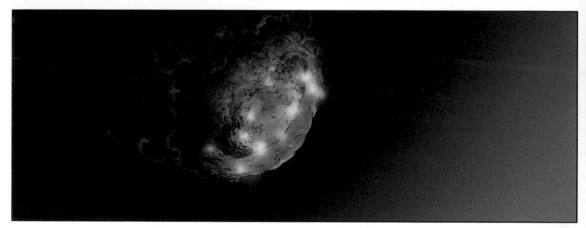

TH-THIS IS THE UTOPIAN. WHERE IS EVERYBODY? WHOEVER'S BEHIND THIS IS IMPERSONATING OUR *TEAMMATES.* I NEED *BACKUP!*

AW, HELL. WOULD YOU *LISTEN* TO HIM? IS HE REALLY SUCH A *DUMB-ASS?*

NOBODY'S IMPERSONATING *ANYONE,* GRAMPS. *WE'RE* YOUR TEAMMATES. DON'T YOU *GET IT?*

WE'RE JUST SICK AND TIRED OF ALL YOUR *BULLSHIT,* MAN... ALWAYS TELLING US WHAT TO DO. ALWAYS *BITCHING* ABOUT US NOT BEING *GOOD ENOUGH.*

I BET YOU WISH YOU'D BEEN *NICER* TO US NOW, HUH?

UGH!

OH MY GOD...

ANEURYSM.

NO!

CHLOE, PLEASE. DON'T MAKE ME FEEL WORSE ABOUT THIS THAN I ALREADY DO...

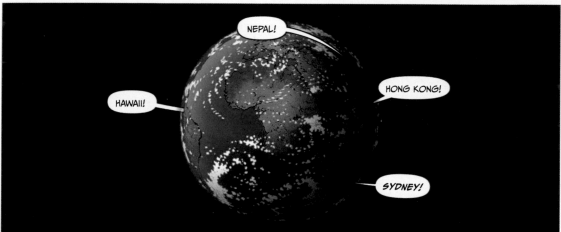

THE ARIZONA DESERT:

EVERYBODY STAND BACK!

B-BRANDON? IS THAT *YOU?*

WH-WHAT'S *HAPPENING?* WHAT ARE THEY *DOING?*

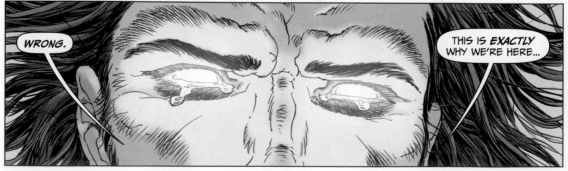

CHAPTER 4

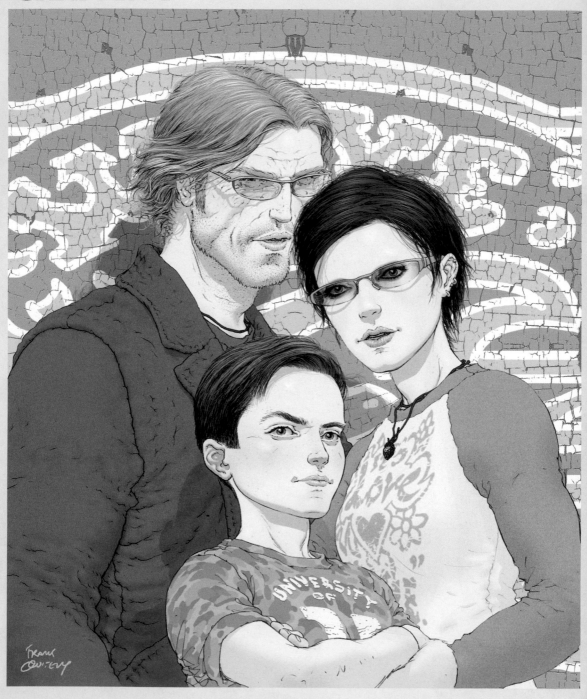

EXACTLY HOW IT LOOKED, GEORGE. RIGHT DOWN TO THE SMALLEST DETAILS.

THE SIGNAL'S COMING FROM THE NORTHWEST HILLS. THAT'S A TWO DAY HIKE EVEN IF WE'RE BRISK SO WE NEED TO MAKE SURE WE'VE GOT PLENTY OF *WATER*.

ARE YOU SURE I CAN'T CARRY THOSE *BAGS* FOR YOU, GRACE?

I THINK YOU FORGET I WAS CAPTAIN OF THE LADIES' *WRESTLING TEAM*, BUSTER. BUT THANKS FOR *ASKING*.

MAYBE ONE OF US SHOULD STAY BEHIND AND KEEP AN EYE ON THE SHIP. I KNOW THE ISLAND *LOOKS* LIKE IT'S SAFE, BUT WE'VE NO WAY HOME IF ANYTHING *HAPPENS* TO IT.

WE'LL BE *FINE*, WALTER. THE ISLAND SAID WE WON'T *NEED* THE SHIP ONCE WE'RE GIVEN THE *GIFTS* WE'VE BEEN PROMISED UP HERE.

AM I THE ONLY ONE FEELING A LITTLE *NERVOUS* ABOUT ALL THESE CRAZY *DREAM MESSAGES* HE'S BEEN GETTING?

QUIT *YAKKING* AND START *HIKING*, SQUIRT. SINCE WHEN HAS YOUR BROTHER BEEN WRONG ABOUT *ANYTHING?*

"IT WASN'T UNTIL LATER THEY REALIZED WHAT THEY WERE HIKING ACROSS.

"WHAT SEEMED LIKE ROCK WAS *ALIEN HARDWARE*. WHAT LOOKED LIKE JUNGLE JUST CENTURIES OF *VEGETATION*.

"THE HILLS THEMSELVES WERE CRISS-CROSSED WITH A SPECIAL METAL THAT NOBODY HAD EVER *SEEN* BEFORE, AND AS THEY CLIMBED IT SOON BECAME OBVIOUS THE ISLAND WAS A *MACHINE*.

"IT HAD BEEN POSITIONED HERE FOR A VERY LONG TIME, WAITING FOR THE PERFECT CANDIDATES AND SHROUDED IN WHAT YOU AND I WOULD CALL A *CLOAKING DEVICE*.

"BUT MOM AND DAD HAD NO IDEA UNTIL THEY MADE THEIR WAY TO THE TOP OF THE TOWER AND GOT TO SEE WHAT DAD HAD BEEN *DREAMING* ABOUT..."

C'MON, MISS SAMPSON. GIVE ME THAT PRETTY *HAND*...

GET OFF MY BACK, GEORGE. I'M NOT GOING TO WARN YOU AGAIN ABOUT THESE STUPID CRACKS.

PIPE DOWN! *BOTH* OF YOU! WE'RE ALL GOING TO NEED OUR *WITS* ONCE WE'RE THROUGH TO THE OTHER SIDE...

DON'T BE SCARED. THESE ARE THE CREATURES WHO CALLED US HERE AND THEY ONLY WANT TO *HELP*.

THEY KNOW OUR COUNTRY IS *DYING* RIGHT NOW AND THEY WANT US TO GO BACK AND MAKE EVERYTHING *RIGHT* AGAIN.

BUT *HOW?*

THEY'RE GOING TO GIVE US *POWERS*, GEORGE. THEY'RE GOING TO MAKE US BETTER THAN ANY OF US COULD EVER *DREAM*.

WE JUST HAVE TO *TRUST* THEM.

AUSTRALIA, 2022:

I *LOVE* THE STORY OF HOW THEY GOT THEIR POWERS. THINGS WERE ALWAYS SO COOL AND *MYSTERIOUS* IN THE OLD DAYS.

DID THEY EVER FIND OUT WHO THE ALIENS *WERE* OR WHY THEY WANTED TO HELP THEM SO MUCH?

TO TELL YOU THE TRUTH, THEY NEVER EVEN FOUND *THE ISLAND* AGAIN, JASON. IT'S LIKE IT ALL JUST APPEARED WHEN WE NEEDED IT MOST AND DISAPPEARED WHEN THINGS WERE BACK *ON TRACK.*

I DOUBT THEY'D EVEN BELIEVE IT *THEMSELVES* IF THEY HADN'T COME HOME WITH ALL THEIR AMAZING POWERS.

WHOSE IDEA WERE THE *COSTUMES,* MOM? WAS THAT GRANDMA'S OR GRANDPA'S?

BOTH, I THINK. THEY WANTED TO *INSPIRE* PEOPLE AND IT REALLY SEEMED TO WORK. THE NEXT FIFTY YEARS WERE A *GOLDEN AGE* FOR AMERICA.

I LOVE THESE STORIES ABOUT THE OLD DAYS. TELL ME SOMETHING ELSE, MOM? WHAT *OTHER STUFF* DID MY GRANDPARENTS GET UP TO?

I'M NOT SURE THERE'RE ANY STORIES LEFT. I MUST HAVE *TOLD* YOU ALL THE GOOD ONES.

SO TELL ME SOMETHING THEY DID WITH THEIR *POWERS.* YOU AND I NEED TO KEEP OURS A *SECRET,* SO IT'S GREAT HEARING ALL THE FEATS THEY WOULD DO WITH *THEIRS.*

...AND THE FUNNY WAYS HE USED TO BEAT HIS *BAD GUYS*. HE NEVER ACTUALLY *HURT* ANYONE, ALWAYS PREFERRING TO DO SOMETHING *CLEVER* AND DEFEAT THEM USING HIS *BRAINS*.

WOW, WHERE DO I EVEN *START?* THERE'S THE SPECIAL BASEBALL DAD MADE SO WE COULD ALL PLAY CATCH IN *THE CLOUDS*...

"BUT I THINK MY FAVORITE THING HAS TO BE THEIR *ENGAGEMENT* STORY. DID I EVER TELL YOU THIS?

"THEY WERE RESCUING MINERS IN SOUTH AMERICA WHEN DAD TOOK A LUMP OF COAL AND SQUEEZED IT SO HARD HE TURNED IT INTO A *DIAMOND*. DID YOU KNOW YOU CAN EVEN *DO* THAT?

OH, SURE. A DIAMOND IS ONLY SUPER CONDENSED GRAPHITE SO IF YOU PICK THE CORRECT ROCK AND APPLY THE APPROPRIATE HEAT AND PRESSURE AN UNPOLISHED DIAMOND IS THE LOGICAL *END RESULT*.

OF COURSE IT IS. SILLY ME!

WHY DO *YOU* THINK THOSE ALIENS GAVE THEM THEIR SUPERPOWERS, MOM? ISN'T IT A LITTLE WEIRD THAT THEY EVEN *KNEW* ABOUT AMERICA?

I DON'T KNOW, JASON. I NEVER REALLY *THINK* ABOUT IT...

...BUT I'M PRETTY SURE IT WASN'T SO THE WORLD COULD LOOK LIKE *THIS*.

I THOUGHT WE HAD A *BAN* ON TALKING ABOUT THE OLD DAYS, CHLOE. YOU'RE ONLY GOING TO GIVE HIM *CRAZY IDEAS.*

THE SUPERPEOPLE KILLED MOM'S *PARENTS*, DAD. THERE'S NOTHING CRAZY ABOUT WANTING *BAD GUYS* BROUGHT TO *JUSTICE.*

THERE IS IF THERE'S ONLY *THREE* OF US, KID. WE HAVE TO BE *REALISTIC* ABOUT ALL THIS AND YOUR MOM KNOWS THAT MORE THAN ANYONE.

HE'S RIGHT, JASON. BRANDON AND UNCLE WALTER DON'T KNOW YOU EXIST RIGHT NOW, AND AS LONG AS WE'RE IN HIDING THERE'S NO REASON THEY *SHOULD.*

THERE'S NOTHING I'D LOVE MORE THAN REVENGE ON THOSE ANIMALS, BUT THE SAFETY OF OUR FAMILY IS THE ONLY THING THAT *MATTERS* NOW.

THEY'LL GET THEIRS IN *THE END*, KID. SCUMBAGS ALWAYS *DO.*

NOW PUT OUT YOUR LIGHT AND TRY TO GET SOME SLEEP. YOU'VE GOT A BIG *SOCCER GAME* TO LOSE IN THE MORNING.

DAD WASN'T KIDDING WHEN HE SAID I HAD TO LOSE. HE KNEW I COULD SCORE A *HUNDRED* GOALS, BUT THE ONLY WAY OF STAYING UNDER THE RADAR WAS ALWAYS BEING A DOOFUS.

OF COURSE, THAT DIDN'T MEAN I COULDN'T HAVE A LITTLE FUN...

WHAT'S THE MATTER, BOYS? *TOO* FAST FOR YOU? I THOUGHT YOU SAID YOU WERE *GOOD* AT THIS GAME?

OH GOD. WHAT'S HE DOING?

DON'T SCORE A GOAL. DON'T SCORE A GOAL. *PLEASE* DON'T SCORE A GOAL...

OOPS!

YAY!

WELL PLAYED, JASON! WELL PLAYED!

MY MOM AND DAD MUST HAVE SEEMED LIKE THE MOST ECCENTRIC PEOPLE IN THE WORLD.

THAT'S *OUR BOY* DOWN THERE!

PARENTS NIGHT WAS ANOTHER BONE OF CONTENTION SINCE I'D BEEN TAUGHT TO HIDE MY GENIUS INTELLECT FROM THE MOMENT I COULD *TALK*...

SO HE'S *STRUGGLING* WITH ENGLISH, ARITHMETIC IS *AVERAGE*, HIS HANDWRITING IS *POOR* AND YOU DON'T REALLY FEEL HE'S PAYING MUCH *ATTENTION?*

CORRECT. JASON'S PROGRESS HAS BEEN *NON-EXISTENT* THIS TERM. THE FIRST TIME IN MY ENTIRE CAREER THAT A PUPIL HAS LEARNED *ABSOLUTELY NOTHING.*

WELL, YOU CAN'T WIN 'EM ALL, MISTER BUTLER. THANKS FOR TRYING. I HOPE YOU HAVE MORE LUCK WITH ALL THE *OTHER* KIDS!

I WAS EVEN ENCOURAGED TO GET BEATEN UP EVERY ONCE IN A WHILE. JUST TO BE ON THE *SAFE SIDE*...

HEY! WHAT'S *GOING ON?*

RUN! IT'S HIS *OLD MAN!*

WAS THAT *OKAY*, DAD? I TRIED MY BEST TO ROLL WITH THE PUNCHES AND MAKE SURE MY SCHOOL PALS DIDN'T BRUISE THEIR *KNUCKLES.*

YOU DID GOOD, BUDDY. IT HONESTLY COULDN'T HAVE LOOKED MORE CONVINCING...

...NOW LET'S GO GET YOU AN ICE CREAM FOR BEING SUCH A GREAT KID.

THE SUPERHEROES HAD TAKEN OVER AMERICA, BUT IT HADN'T WORKED OUT AS WELL AS THEY'D *HOPED.*

THEY'D MANAGED TO FIX A *COUPLE* OF PROBLEMS, BUT THINGS ON THE WHOLE HAD BEEN PRETTY *CATASTROPHIC* AND EVEN IN AUSTRALIA WE WERE FEELING THE *IMPACT.*

RECLAIM

EUROPE HAD BEEN PARTICULARLY AFFECTED, A MILLION ASYLUM SEEKERS GIVEN *TEMPORARY RESIDENCE*, MAKING IT NICE AND EASY FOR US TO HIDE AMONG THE MASSES.

WHY DO YOU ALWAYS CARRY YOUR *POWER ROD*, DAD? AREN'T YOU WORRIED YOU'LL GET SEARCHED BY THE *COPS* SOMETIME?

YEAH, BUT THEY'RE LOOKING FOR SUPERS TWENTY-FOUR-SEVEN AND I NEED TO BE ABLE TO *DEFEND* MYSELF, PAL.

IS IT TRUE YOUR DAD BUILT *THAT THING* FROM *SCRATCH?*

YEP. PAPA GEORGE CUSTOMIZED IT FROM AN OLD *FLASHLIGHT* I HAD. HE SAID HE FELT BAD I DIDN'T HAVE ANY POWERS SO HE MADE ME SOMETHING THAT SIMULATED *HIS.*

PEOPLE ALWAYS SAY WHAT A MONSTER HE WAS, BUT HE MUST HAVE HAD A *GOOD SIDE* TO THINK ABOUT STUFF LIKE *THAT.*

IT'S WEIRD HE USED TO BE BEST FRIENDS WITH *MOM'S* DAD. WHY DO YOU THINK THE TWO OF THEM *FELL OUT?*

WELL, SOMETIMES BEST FRIENDS CAN MAKE WORST OF ENEMIES, KID. IT'S ALL ABOUT *GIRLS* AND *ADULT STUFF* SO I'LL FILL YOU IN WHEN BOTH OF US AREN'T *BLUSHING.*

WHAT'S GOING ON *HERE?*

CHEMICAL PLANT IN *KURNELL,* MAN. THEY'VE BEEN FIGHTING A FIRE FOR AN HOUR AND A HALF, BUT IT'S SUPPOSED TO BE *GETTING WORSE* IF ANYTHING.

KURNELL? ISN'T THAT LIKE *TWENTY MILES* AWAY?

THAT'S HOW *DESPERATE* THEY ARE. THEY'RE CALLING IN CREWS FROM HALF THE REGION, BUT THE RADIO SAYS THEY'RE BARELY MAKING A *DENT.*

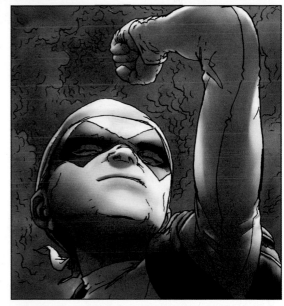

MAN, THAT'S THE WEIRDEST THING I EVER SAW IN MY LIFE. YOU SEE THE WAY THAT THUNDERCLOUD JUST CAME OUT OF *NOWHERE?*

FREAKY.

SEE, THAT'S WHAT I'M ALWAYS TELLING YOUR *MOM.* SUPERHEROES *THINK* THEY NEED TO STICK THEIR NOSES INTO THINGS, BUT LIFE HAS A WAY OF WORKING *ITSELF* OUT.

I COULDN'T AGREE *MORE,* DAD.

NOW LET'S GO HOME SO YOU CAN FAKE FLUNKING YOUR *HOMEWORK.*

SAY NO

35

WASHINGTON D.C. :

BRANDON, COME AWAY FROM THE WINDOW AND *IGNORE* THOSE IDIOTS. YOU'RE SUPPOSED TO BE CELEBRATING *NINE YEARS* IN *POWER.*

FOOD BANKS? RIOTS IN THE STREETS? I'M NOT REALLY SURE THERE'S ANYTHING TO *CELEBRATE*, UNCLE WALTER.

THIS ISN'T HOW THINGS WERE SUPPOSED TO *TURN OUT*, MAN. THE PLAN WAS TO MAKE THINGS *BETTER* FOR EVERYONE, BUT IT'S ALL JUST BEEN CONSTANT *GRIEF.*

OH, COME ON. WHERE WAS AMERICA GOING BEFORE *WE* TOOK OVER?

YES, THERE'VE BEEN SETBACKS WITH JOBS AND HOMES, BUT WE'RE OVERTURNING AN *ENTIRE CONSTITUTION* HERE. IT'S ONLY NATURAL THERE ARE GOING TO BE A FEW BUMPS ON *THE ROAD.*

CHAPTER 5

MELBOURNE:

GOOD MORNING, EVERYONE. NO NEED TO BE ALARMED.

I'D LIKE TO SPEAK WITH A *MISS JOAN WILSON*, IF YOU'LL PARDON THE INTERRUPTION.

ME?

THAT'S RIGHT, MISS WILSON. IF YOU'D CARE TO COME AND JOIN ME AT THE FRONT. I ONLY NEED TO ASK A FEW *SIMPLE QUESTIONS.*

UH, OKAY. J-JUST SEEMS A LITTLE WEIRD, THAT'S ALL.

I'M SURE YOU ALREADY KNOW WHO I AM, BUT JUST IN CASE YOU DON'T...

...MY NAME IS MAJOR BARNABAS WOLFE AND IT'S MY RESPONSIBILITY TO FIND ANY *UNLICENSED SUPERHUMANS* HIDING AT HOME OR HERE IN A *FOREIGN TERRITORY.*

I... I DON'T UNDERSTAND. WHAT'S THAT GOT TO DO WITH ME? I'M JUST A *CLAIMS SUPERVISOR.*

I'LL BE THE JUDGE OF THAT, IF YOU DON'T MIND, MISS WILSON.

NOW THE GOVERNMENT BACK HOME IS PUSHING THROUGH *RADICAL REFORMS* AND WE HAVE TO BE VIGILANT ABOUT ANY *SUPERPOWERED REBELS* WHO MIGHT BE HIDING ABROAD.

I JUST WANT TO RUN THROUGH A FEW *INCONSISTENCIES* WE'VE NOTED WITH REGARDS TO YOUR FILE. I TRUST THIS ISN'T A *PROBLEM?*

NO, NOT AT ALL. I COMPLETELY UNDERSTAND. PLEASE... ASK ME ANYTHING YOU LIKE.

YOU PROBABLY DON'T *REMEMBER* ME. I NEVER REALLY MADE MUCH OF AN IMPRESSION AS *THE MOLECULE MASTER*, DESPITE THESE ELABORATE SUPERPOWERS.

YES, I COULD REARRANGE THE STRUCTURE OF INORGANIC MATTER, BUT I DIDN'T REALLY *ENJOY* FIGHTING CRIME AND I WASN'T REALLY *DASHING* ENOUGH FOR *THE MAGAZINES.*

BUT HUNTING DOWN THREATS TO THE STATE? TRACKING DOWN SUPER CRIMINALS AND SENDING THEM TO THE *SUPERMAX?* I THINK I'VE FINALLY FOUND MY *CALLING.*

CONTROL, THIS IS MAJOR WOLFE WITH THE *ANTI-TERROR UNIT...*

...IT ISN'T THE PRIZE WE WERE *HOPING* FOR, BUT I'VE BAGGED US ANOTHER *MISSING FELON.*

I LOVE COMING UP WITH SILLY EXCUSES TO GET OUT OF SCHOOL AND HELP WITH *EMERGENCIES*.

PRETENDING TO GET SEASICK WHILE READING *MOBY-DICK* GAVE ME A CHANCE TO RESCUE A *SKY DIVER* AND PULL A TROUBLED *CRUISE SHIP* INTO SAFER WATERS.

I DON'T REALLY MIND THE OTHER KIDS THINKING I'M A WET BLANKET.

A CLUMSY ALTER EGO IS A USEFUL TOOL FOR ANY SUPERHERO AND IF MY *GRANDFATHER* DIDN'T MIND TRIPPING OVER HIS SHOELACES, I DON'T SEE WHY IT SHOULD BOTHER *ME*.

BESIDES, NOT HAVING ANY FRIENDS TO HANG OUT WITH MEANS I CAN SPEND MY LUNCH BREAKS UP HERE WORKING ON MY *SECRET PROJECT*.

I'VE GOT MY FLIGHT TIME HERE AND BACK DOWN TO *NINETEEN MINUTES* AS OF YESTERDAY. THAT'S *PLENTY* OF TIME TO GET BACK FOR THE FIRST CLASS OF THE *AFTERNOON*.

OH NO.

I'M DYING TO HEAR THE EXPLANATION FOR *THIS* ONE...

SAN FRANCISCO:

IS IT AS BAD AS IT LOOKED ON *TV?*

ACTUALLY, IT MIGHT BE A LITTLE WORSE. BUT IF YOU DON'T EXPERIMENT WITH NEW IDEAS YOU'RE GOING TO BE RELIANT ON *GAS* AND *OIL* FOREVER.

EXACTLY. JUST REMEMBER THAT ALL THESE PEOPLE COMPLAINING WOULD HAVE BEEN FIRST IN LINE FOR YOUR *FREE ELECTRICITY PLAN,* WALTER.

I MIGHT HAVE SOMETHING TO CHEER YOU UP HERE ANYWAY. AS YOU PROBABLY HEARD, WE DIDN'T FIND CHLOE, BUT THERE'S STILL AN ODD NUMBER OF *LAST-MINUTE RESCUES* GOING ON OUT HERE.

SKYSCRAPER DIDN'T HAVE THE *RANGE* FOR THESE FEATS SO I TOLD TECHNICAL TO BE FORENSIC WITH THE SATELLITE FOOTAGE.

THE BOY COVERED HIS TRACKS VERY WELL, BUT THERE'S ALWAYS *SOME* SMALL DETAIL THEY FORGET. IN HIS CASE, A REFLECTION IN A SINGLE *RAIN DROP.*

THE SCHOOL BUS ROUTE:

THE *DOOR* FELL OFF. YOU *UNDERSTAND?*

NOT A WORD TO *ANYONE.*

I'M SORRY, MOM, BUT I CAN'T STAND BACK IF PEOPLE *NEED HELP...*

...I'VE GOT TOO MUCH OF MY *GRANDFATHER* IN ME.

BE SURE TO
GIVE HIM MY
REGARDS.

MOMMY ISN'T *COMING,* LITTLE MAN. WHEREVER SHE IS, SHE'S HARDLY GOING TO HEAR YOU ALL THE WAY OUT *HERE.*

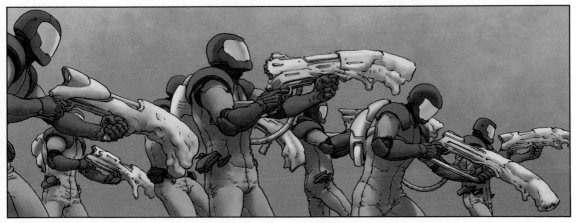

HOLY SHIT...

...ISN'T THAT YOUR WIFE ON TV?

ALPHA TEAM! THREE ROUNDS ON MY COMMAND!

DON'T WORRY, MOM. THEY'LL HAVE TO GET THROUGH *ME* FIRST.

THIS KID'S *HILARIOUS.*

WEAPONS CHARGED, BOYS!

GET THE HELL AWAY FROM MY SON!

OH, CHLOE! LOOK AT YOU *NOW!* SMOKED OUT OF HIDING TO SAVE YOUR *LITTLE BOY...*

WELL, IT LOOKS LIKE YOU'VE BITTEN OFF MORE THAN YOU CAN CHEW, MY DEAR.

THERE'S *HUNDREDS* OF US HERE AND MORE ON THE *WAY.* DO YOU REALLY THINK SOME USELESS PARTY GIRL STANDS A CHANCE AGAINST *US?*

THINGS HAVE *CHANGED,* BAKNABAS. I'M NOT A *LITTLE GIRL* ANYMORE.

MY *MOM* WAS A SUPERHERO. MY *DAD* WAS A SUPERHERO...

...THAT MEANS I WON THIS FIGHT BEFORE YOU GOT OUT OF BED.

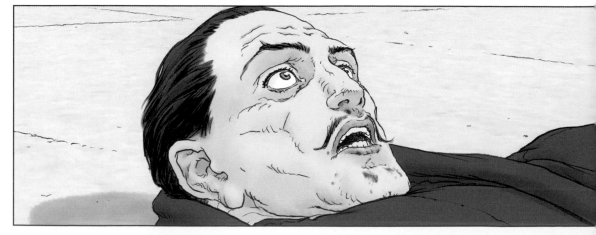

CHLOE'S FRIENDS:

OH MY GOD. TOO *AWESOME*.

LIVE

...live from Sydney... LiveLink

JASON'S FRIENDS:

UH, YOU DON'T THINK JASON'LL BE *MAD* AT US, DO YOU?

THE INDO-US TRADE TALKS:

MISTER SAMPSON, COULD I HAVE A WORD?

WHAT THE HELL DID YOU JUST SAY TO ME?

THE NORTH POLE:

"OKAY, DADDY. YOU CAN OPEN YOUR EYES...

...HOW DOES CHLOE LOOK IN HER *SECRET IDENTITY?*

LIKE SHE'S GOING TO SAVE THE WORLD ONE DAY.

TO BE CONTINUED

ISSUE 2 VARIANT
BRYAN HITCH
COLOR BY JOHN RAUCH

ISSUE 2 VARIANT
AMY REEDER

ISSUE 5 VARIANT
DUNCAN FEGREDO
COLOR BY PETER DOHERTY

GIANT SIZE EDITION
JOHN CASSADAY
COLOR BY PETER DOHERTY

MARK MILLAR

Mark Millar is the *New York Times* bestselling author of *Kick-Ass*, *Wanted*, and *Kingsman: The Secret Service*, all of which have been adapted into Hollywood franchises.

His DC Comics work includes the seminal *Superman: Red Son*. At Marvel Comics he created *The Ultimates*, which was selected by *Time* magazine as the comic book of the decade, and was described by screenwriter Zak Penn as his major inspiration for *The Avengers* movie. Millar also created *Wolverine: Old Man Logan* and *Civil War*, Marvel's two biggest-selling graphic novels ever. *Civil War* was the basis of the *Captain America: Civil War* movie, and *Old Man Logan* was the inspiration for Fox's *Logan* movie in 2017.

Mark has been an executive producer on all his movies, and for four years worked as a creative consultant to Fox Studios on their Marvel slate of movies. In 2017, Netflix bought Millarworld in the company's first ever acquisition, and employed Mark as President of a new division to create comics, TV shows, and movies. His much-anticipated autobiography, *The Man With the Golden Brain*, will be published next year.

FRANK QUITELY

Frank Quitely is a Scottish comic book artist. He is best known for his frequent collaborations with Grant Morrison on titles such as *New X-Men, We3, All-Star Superman,* and *Batman and Robin,* as well as his work with Mark Millar on *The Authority* and *Jupiter's Legacy.*

Frank Quitely spent the first three years of his comic book career in the independently-published Scottish adult humor anthology *Electric Soup,* learning the basics of writing, drawing and lettering his own black and white strip, *The Greens.*

Leaving the writing behind, he spent a further two years painting the futuristic western *Missionary Man* and Japanese sci-fi strip *Shimura,* both for the poular UK anthology *Judge Dredd Megazine.*

The next five years were mostly spent at DC, producing ten black and white strips for Paradox Press' *The Big Books*, six shorts and two mini-series for Vertigo, including *Flex Mentallo,* and a selection of one-shots, original graphic novels and ongoing series at DCU and Wildstorm, including *Batman, JLA* and *The Authority.*

After two years on *New X-Men* at Marvel, he headed back to Vertigo for a fully painted *Sandman* short, and the creator-owned mini-series *We3,* followed by *All-Star Superman, Batman and Robin, New Gods,* and *Pax Americana,* all for DC Comics.

When not digitally painting covers or dabbling in small press ventures, he's occasionally to be found designing characters for animation, and producing artwork for CD covers and Posters.

He currently has *Jupiter's Legacy* Volume Two and several smaller creator-owned projects in the pipeline.

PETER DOHERTY

Peter's first work in comics was during 1990, providing painted artwork for the John Wagner-written *"Young Death: The Boyhood of a Super-fiend"*, published in the first year of the *Judge Dredd Megazine*. For the next few years he painted art for a number of Judge Dredd stories.

During the closing years of the 90s he worked for several comics publishers, most notably DC/Vertigo, and branched out into illustration, TV, and movie work.

A year as an in-house concept artist at a games company revealed to Peter that he didn't much like having bosses, and he returned to freelancing. Working digitally for the first time opened the door to coloring work, firstly on the Grant Morrison/Cameron Stewart *Seaguy,* and with Geof Darrow on his creation *The Shaolin Cowboy* .

Over the last decade he's balanced working on projects both as the sole artist and as a coloring collaborator with other artists, most recently with his old friends, Frank Quitely and Duncan Fegredo, on the Millarworld projects *Jupiter's Legacy* and *MPH,* respectively.

ROB MILLER

Since stumbling onto the Glasgow comic scene in 2005 (via architecture and the underground title *Khaki Shorts*), Rob Miller has been fortunate enough to assist Frank Quitely on his recent genre-defining works with Mark Millar and Grant Morrison.

Working from Jamie Grant's highly regarded Hope Street Studios has allowed him to collaborate with other Scottish comics professionals, including Alan Grant and Alex Ronald, as well as providing the opportunity to publish prized collections of some of his very favorite local underground artists – Dave Alexander, Hugh "Shug '90" McKenna and John Miller – under his own Braw Books imprint.

NICOLE BOOSE

Nicole Boose began her comics career as an assistant editor for Harris Comics' *Vampirella,* before joining the editorial staff at Marvel Comics. There, she edited titles including *Cable & Deadpool, Invincible Iron Man,* and Stephen King's *Dark Tower* adaptations, and oversaw Marvel's line of custom comic publications.

Since 2008, Nicole has worked as a freelance editor and consultant in the comics industry, with editorial credits that include the Millarworld titles *Superior, Super Crooks, Jupiter's Legacy, MPH, Starlight,* and *Chrononauts.* Nicole is also Communications Manager for Comics Experience, an online school and community for comic creators.